Fundamentalism—What Every Catholic Needs to Know

Fundamentalism—
What Every Catholic
Needs to Know

Anthony E. Gilles

Nihil Obstat: Rev. Hilarion Kistner, O.F.M.
                 Rev. John J. Jennings

Imprimi Potest: Rev. Jeremy Harrington, O.F.M.
                 Provincial

Imprimatur: +James H. Garland, V.G.
                 Archdiocese of Cincinnati
                 December 10, 1984

Book design and cover by Julie Lonneman.

SBN 0-89716-043-8

Contents

Introduction   1

Chapter One: What Is Fundamentalism?   7

Three Groups of Fundamentalists   8
The History of Fundamentalism   11
Common Fundamentalist Tendencies   14
Fundamentalism's Good Points   23

Chapter Two: Who's Right About the Bible?   25

'Inspiration' and 'Inerrancy': The Catholic View   28
'Inspiration' and 'Inerrancy': The Fundamentalist
   View   34
How We Got Today's Bible   36

Chapter Three: What Catholics Believe—Responding to
                Fundamentalist Challenges   41

'Have You Been Saved?'   41
'Mary Couldn't Have Been a Virgin'   46
'Call No One on Earth Your Father'   48
'The Mass Is Not a Sacrifice'   49
'One Is Saved by Faith Alone'   51
'Show Me the Pope, the Catholic Church and the Trinity
   in the Bible'   53
'Are You Ready for the Rapture?'   56

Conclusion   61

Introduction

I was born in a small Kentucky town which, because of its large Catholic population, was unique in its day. Even though the entire population of my hometown was only about 35,000, there were so many Catholics living there that we had our own bishop.

The reason for this unusually large number of Catholics in that small Kentucky town was Jean Baptiste Lamy. Many years before my birth that great French missionary had passed through the area with a group of Ursuline nuns and established a firm Catholic foundation in this part of Kentucky. (This is the same—and eventual Archbishop—Lamy whose life story is told by Willa Cather in her famous novel, *Death Comes for the Archbishop*.)

Because of Jean Baptiste Lamy, Catholicism—at least in my corner of Kentucky—was never seen as a foreign or alien religion in a sea of Protestantism. Each Sunday morning I would go with my parents to the massive and beautiful St. Stephen's Cathedral and wave to my Protestant friends across the street who went, dressed in coat and tie, to the equally massive and beautiful First Baptist Church. Although we knew there were differences between us, these differences never served to divide us. (My earliest idea about what distinguished Catholics and Protestants was the fact that Protestants always dressed up for church while Catholics rarely did.)

Some time after my 10th birthday, however, my father

accepted a job in Nashville, Tennessee. We left our small Kentucky town for what I thought would be "the big city." There I expected to find sophisticated and exciting people who would stimulate my thinking in new and challenging directions.

My hopes were soon dashed.

On the first Saturday morning following our move, two ladies carrying Bibles approached our house and engaged my mother in conversation. After a few moments of chitchat, one of the ladies asked the question which summarized the purpose of their visit: "And where do you folks plan to go to church?"

To my mother there was never any "plan" about it. We were going to attend Christ the King Catholic Church since that was the parish in which we lived. Upon this news the ladies' stiff smiles turned to frozen grimaces. That was the first indication I can remember that not all Protestants accepted my Catholic beliefs with the "live-and-let-live" attitude I had known in western Kentucky. This was also my first contact with Protestant *fundamentalists*. What I didn't realize at the time was that life as a Southern Catholic, life in the "Bible Belt," would become a constant confrontation with fundamentalists.

First of all, there were the many TV and radio programs which promoted anti-Catholicism. In high school I used to watch a program called *Back to the Bible* with the Reverend J. Basil Mull. *Back to the Bible* was sponsored by a local coffee company, and Reverend Mull once told us the Lord himself appeared in a dream to tell the Reverend his audience should purchase the sponsor's coffee.

The Reverend J. Basil Mull loved to use the word *prove* during his talks. He could "prove" this and "prove" that about the Bible, but in particular he could "prove" that the Catholic Church was the Whore of Babylon and that the Pope was the Antichrist. The good Reverend always ended his programs by saying, "And I invite any Romanist in the audience to come down and debate me on anything I have discussed today."

Then there were the fundamentalist tracts and pamphlets which constantly turned up in the vestibules of Catholic churches (as well as in almost every public building in town). These tracts likewise "proved" from the Bible the evil of the Catholic Church and the truth of the writer's particular brand of "Christianity." This quite open and public prejudice against Catholicism during my teenage years was, I assume, simply

2

taken for granted by the rest of the population.

During the 1960 presidential election, one of the largest Churches in our city ran a series of ads promoting a film entitled *Kennedy Can Be Defeated*. The fact that my teenage friends and I plastered the front doors of the church with Kennedy-Johnson stickers may have helped to deter the institution from showing its film.

During my freshman year at the University of Tennessee, attendance was required for the annual "convocation," a three-day series of meetings at which a notable fundamentalist preacher would harangue us about various "truths" of the Bible. It was not until the 1970's that these convocations were finally canceled by the university administration.

Walking a Tightrope

As a Catholic growing up in the Bible Belt, I experienced firsthand the antagonism fundamentalists feel toward the Catholic religion. Yet in examining fundamentalist doctrines, I find that many of them are doctrines in which I myself believe. I believe, as fundamentalists do, in the virgin birth of Jesus, the physical resurrection of Jesus, salvation through Jesus' death and resurrection, that Jesus will come again in glory and triumph, and that the Bible is the inspired Word of God.

Fundamentalists may be surprised to learn that I first became acquainted with all of these doctrines in the first grade in parochial school, when the nuns began to teach them to me. Many of the beliefs which fundamentalists cherish are in fact "fundamentals" of Roman Catholicism.

In writing a book about *fundamentalism* from a critical point of view, I feel, therefore, a little like someone walking a tightrope. I fear that I may come across as attacking the *fundamentals* of Christian belief.

Please understand that an attack on these fundamentals is the last thing on my mind. I will critique the way in which some fundamentalists misuse, misunderstand and misappropriate the fundamentals of the Christian faith. But my words of criticism in the pages ahead are directed at fundamental*ism*, not at the fundamentals.

There is thus a great distinction to be made between the

3

words *fundamental* and *fundamentalism*. This distinction is similar, for example, to the difference between the words *moral* and *moralism* (or *moralist*); or between the words *legal* and *legalism* (or *legalist*). It's the *ism* and the *ist* that cause the problem.

Fundamental*ism* connotes a distortion—a hyperextension, one might say—of the fundamentals. Attaching *ist* and *ism* to *fundamental* suggests adhering to doctrines for their own sake, without seeing their purpose. This is precisely the problem with fundamentalism: It is such an absorption and fascination with doctrine that it actually distorts doctrinal meaning and significance. Fundamentalists are so preoccupied with religious doctrine that they have made it an end in itself rather than a means to an end. They are so preoccupied with the trees that they can't see the forest.

I often illustrate this point to my fundamentalist friends by reminding them that when they go to heaven they will not worship a huge granite replica of a Bible—any more than we Catholics will worship a huge replica of Vatican City.

What This Book Is Not

My earlier encounters with religious extremism have provided much of the background for this book. In my memory I can still see many harsh faces and judgmental stares. I can still sense the great, gloomy pessimism about life which pervaded the fundamentalist South of my upbringing. I hope, nonetheless, that my personal experience will not turn the following chapters into a diatribe against fundamentalists.

Neither do I intend this book as a criticism of Protestantism. Many Protestant denominations today also come under attack from fundamentalist groups. Many Protestants have condemned the anti-Catholic bigotry which underlies the cruder forms of fundamentalism. These Protestants are as repulsed as Catholics by the tactics of some fundamentalists. There is thus a great distinction to be made between the word *Protestant* and the word *fundamentalist*.

Further, I do not intend in this book to establish Catholicism as the supreme religious system. This book is not a quick course in Catholic apologetics. Those of you who went through 12 years of Catholic education may feel (as I do) that

4

the neat arguments outlined to "prove" the truths of the Catholic faith never really did much good and, further, that this "apologetic" approach is too close to the tactics of the fundamentalists for comfort.

What This Book Promises

Now that I have said what this book is *not*, let me summarize briefly what it *is*. It is intended for Catholics (as well as for non-fundamentalist Protestants) who feel perplexed and frustrated by their confrontation with fundamentalists. And its purpose is threefold:

1) *To provide a practical guide for understanding fundamentalism as it presents itself in daily life.* My approach in developing this "working definition" will be largely anecdotal—that is, based on my own experiences with fundamentalism—rather than academic and abstract.

2) *To contrast the Catholic and the fundamentalist views of the Bible*—by showing how the Bible evolved historically. I will also discuss the essential role of Scripture scholarship in helping us appreciate the Bible's message for today.

3) *To help Catholics answer fundamentalist challenges to certain Catholic beliefs.* Thus I will be clarifying the Catholic understanding of certain faith issues. Even those readers not regularly challenged by fundamentalist ideas will, I trust, appreciate this clarification of Catholic beliefs.

I hope this critique of fundamental*ism* helps to reaffirm your own belief in the fundamentals of our Christian faith. This faith—in a Father who loves his wayward people throughout history, in a God-man who died and rose from the dead to redeem us, in a Holy Spirit who continues to counsel and inspire us—will always remain a great mystery. Yet we have a strong Church tradition which helps interpret this mystery so we can better live out our Christian beliefs. May the faith we live be not a distortion or caricature of the faith handed down to us through the ages, but may it rather reflect "…the sound doctrines of our Lord Jesus Christ and the teaching proper to true religion…" (1 Timothy 6:3).

CHAPTER ONE

What Is Fundamentalism?

Fundamentalism is a universal problem in all religions. Wherever die-hard and rigid adherence to doctrine for its own sake exists, there exists a fundamentalist. This is so whether the fundamentalist is Protestant, Catholic, Jewish, Moslem or Buddhist.

Because fundamentalism is not really a doctrine in itself so much as a way of looking at doctrine, it is not possible to make a clean distinction between *us* (the non-fundamentalists) and *them* (the fundamentalists). Therefore I had better prepare my Catholic readers for something of a challenge. Even though the focus in this book will be Protestant fundamentalism, certain aspects of Catholicism evidence some of the very fundamentalist tendencies which I will criticize in the pages ahead.

Perhaps one of the most well-known recent illustrations of fundamentalism is the religious system of the infamous Ayatollah Khomeini. The Ayatollah is a true fundamentalist in every sense of the word, literally interpreting the Koran and shaping it to his own narrow viewpoint, all in the name of God and God's justice. When a thief is convicted in Iran, the Ayatollah decrees that his hand be cut off. Fornication and adultery are capital offenses. Women are to keep their "shameful bodies" covered from head to foot.

If we think about it honestly, we have had many Ayatollahs—both Catholic and Protestant—in the Christian tradition. Likewise, many today who call themselves Christians really ascribe more to the belief system of the Ayatollah than they do to the gospel of Jesus Christ. Such Christians demand an eye for an eye instead of mercy for convicted criminals. Instead of loving their enemies as Jesus commanded, they insist on matching the hated Russians step for step in an arms race which threatens to destroy all life on earth.

If we probe into our own hearts, each of us will discover a little bit of the fundamentalist. We all find it much safer to relate to doctrines than to a living God. We all—Protestant and Catholic—love to use dogmatic warfare as a sort of smoke screen to avoid the real issue—living a Christlike life. I hope, therefore, that this critique of fundamentalism can also be a self-critique of the fundamentalist tendencies within our own religious lives.

Three Groups of Fundamentalists

I'm sure you've heard the popular expression, "There are doctors and then there are doctors," or, "There are lawyers and then there are lawyers." In the same sense, there are fundamentalists and then there are fundamentalists. Not all fundamentalists think alike any more than all Catholics think alike. Given that caution, we can distinguish three groups of fundamentalists:

1) The 'lunatic fringe'

This first type of fundamentalist is exemplified by the Jack Chick Comic Books which are popular in some fundamentalist circles. For those who have not had the misfortune of seeing these publications, they are gory, mindless, bigoted tracts whose chief purpose is to prove that Catholicism is not Christian and that all Catholics are going to hell. Moreover, they are irreparably ignorant about Catholicism and Christianity in general.

As I am writing I have before me a scene from *Alberto*, one of the most popular of the Chick publications. In one scene a Catholic woman is lying on her deathbed. Suddenly, she becomes wide-eyed and horrified as she stares off into the distance, saying that she sees horrible monsters coming to get her. Great beads of sweat roll down her face as she leaves this mortal existence for everlasting damnation—the punishment to which God has consigned her for her Catholic beliefs.

Also a favorite theme in these tracts is the great Catholic

"conspiracy" against the world. In another scene in *Alberto* one reads that the Pope has a computer which has the name, address and phone number of every Protestant in the world. Other illustrations show convents and parish rectories with connecting tunnels where priests and nuns are said to have love affairs. (To the side of the tunnels are stacked the bones of the babies resulting from these alleged affairs.)

Such publications (and they are much more prevalent than one might imagine) depict the workings of extremely prejudiced and misinformed writers and illustrators. There is obviously no possibility for a Catholic to dialogue with anyone who takes these tracts seriously. One can only hope that the Chick publishers and their disciples never achieve any political influence in this country.

2) The 'sophisticated bigot'

This next type of fundamentalist is represented by media stars for whom anti-Catholicism is a multi-million-dollar business.

An illustration of this second type of fundamentalism occurred recently in Dallas, where a fundamentalist school canceled a football game when it accidentally discovered that its opponent was a Catholic institution. I wonder if the trustees of that school are consistent in their principles and place signs in their hardware stores and banks which say, "We don't accept Catholic money."

Representatives of this second group of fundamentalism may not be as extreme as representatives of the first, but there is equally small possibility for dialogue between them and Catholics. Adherents to these first two types of fundamentalism are so hostile to Catholicism, and so threatened by any suggestion that their beliefs are not the only possible beliefs, that any real dialogue with them is pointless.

My own experience as a Southern Catholic has revealed this futility on countless occasions. Recently, for example, a young man in my exercise club was wearing a T-shirt proclaiming, "Jesus saves, the Pope enslaves." I approached the young man and told him that I found his shirt offensive and asked him please not to wear it in the future. I was met with the standard fundamentalist reply of cliches, slogans and memorized jargon. Instead of entering into a dialogue over my feelings about his shirt, or trying to listen to what I was saying, he simply began to run off a long list of unrelated Scripture quotations.

3) The 'informed moderate'

This third type of fundamentalism is quite different from the first two and dialogue with representatives of this third group is possible. Like the second group, this group is represented by media stars, but this third group uses the media in a positive way to promote the gospel. Representatives of this third group include such people as Billy Graham and Pat Robertson. While I don't agree with everything that members of this third group of fundamentalists believe, there is no doubt that they are sincere and good Christians who are doing a lot of good for many people.

A principal distinction between this group of fundamentalists and the first two is that the third group will honestly communicate with Catholics. I know this from firsthand experience. I once wrote a somewhat critical letter to Pat Robertson concerning a report that he had displayed some of the Jack Chick publications on his nationwide television program, the *700 Club*.

I received a prompt, well-written and very satisfactory response from Mr. Robertson. He stated that he had not known that any of the Jack Chick tracts had made their way into his institution, and that he would see to it that they were not allowed in the future. He closed by telling me about an upcoming program he had planned on the Pope's visit to the United States.

Included in this third group is a wide variety of Christians who refer to themselves as "evangelicals." (Actually, no one seems to *want* to be called a "fundamentalist.") Many of these evangelicals adopt and follow certain fundamentalist positions; thus there is often little *doctrinal* distinction between these evangelicals and the first two groups of fundamentalists. These evangelicals, however, are much more Christian in their approach to Catholics than the first two groups I have mentioned and, by and large, they are much better educated and informed.

The evangelical thrust in fundamentalism has given rise to what is really a new denomination in America—what we could call the "nondenominational denomination." We see churches of this denomination springing up everywhere today; they seem to fill a real need among today's Christians.

An example of the thought of this educated evangelical thrust within fundamentalism may be found in the magazine *Christianity Today*. In this magazine one finds a balanced, reasoned and well-written exposition of evangelical fundamentalist doctrine. Although the magazine certainly does not accept Catholicism, it is not "anti-Catholic" in a pejorative sense and, in fact, seems to have a spirit of openness towards dialogue with Catholics.

Obviously *some* fundamentalists will not dialogue with us at all, and we should recognize this sad fact at the beginning. We will be able to work with and learn from other fundamentalists, however, despite our very real differences in approach to the fundamentals of Christianity. Even though some fundamentalists simply refuse to accept Catholics, this should not deter us from trying to involve other fundamentalists—those of the third group—in dialogue, so that we Christians may constantly seek to fulfill the Lord's prayer "that all may be one" (John 17:21).

The History of Fundamentalism

In order to grasp the meaning of fundamentalism today, we need to look at its origins. American Protestant fundamentalism really began as a reaction to a reaction. Let's look at what that means.

Around the turn of the last century certain new ideas seemed to threaten traditional Christian doctrines. In particular, the writings of Charles Darwin, Sigmund Freud, Friedrich Nietzsche and Karl Marx all posed a real challenge to traditional Christianity.

Darwin's scientific findings asserted that the earth was much older than a literal reading of the Bible would allow. Freud's psychoanalytic approach tended to relativize moral actions. Nietzsche, with his teaching of the "transvaluation of all values," likewise sought to abolish absolutes, particularly the absolutist tendencies he saw in Christianity. Marx, who saw Christianity's belief in an afterlife as simply a means by which the rich oppressed the poor, called for the establishment of an earthly utopia in a classless society.

In response to these challenges to traditional Christianity, a school of Christian thinkers called *Modernists* arose among both Protestants and Catholics. Catholic Modernists were simply squelched—to put it bluntly—by the Vatican and ordered not to speculate on any possibility of conciliation between Christianity and the four currents of thought mentioned above.

Protestant Modernists, on the other hand, were free to speculate on the possibility that Christianity could adapt its traditional understanding of the Bible. They took a more conciliatory view of the findings of the new science and philosophy.

Fundamentalism arose as a reaction to the Modernist movement within Protestantism. The name *fundamentalism* stems from several booklets written by various persons between 1909 and 1915 and collectively called *The Fundamentals: A Testimony to the Truth.*

In the face of the Modernist challenge these fundamentalists held strictly to the following positions: the literal inerrancy of the Bible, the virgin birth of Jesus, the physical resurrection of Jesus, the substitutionary theory of the atonement, and the imminent, physical Second Coming of Christ.

Because American fundamentalism arose principally as a *reaction* to Modernism, its early existence was based on negating—being against—another religious position. Ever since that time fundamentalism has maintained this spirit of negativism—of being in *opposition* to something else.

We can distinguish three "phases" in the fundamentalist movement in the United States. (The word *phase* is not quite accurate since it suggests that one period stopped and another period began. In actuality the three phases which we will discuss are all still present in fundamentalism today.)

1) First phase: 'warfare' mentality

This first phase is characterized by the fundamentalist activity which took place between 1900 and 1930. This phase saw the rise of tent meetings, revivals and the wholesale rejection by fundamentalists of many traditional Protestant denominations.

Fundamentalists during this phase taught that the "liberal" Protestant denominations had turned their back on the Bible and had thus become like "the world." (Of course, there was never any doubt that Catholicism in its entirety was likewise to be condemned.)

This first phase is characterized by the "warfare" mentality exemplified in the Scopes trial in Dayton, Tennessee, where the issue of creation versus evolution was first disputed in a court of law. This same warfare mentality still characterizes certain fundamentalist groups today.

2) Second phase: 'nondenominational denomination'

During this second phase, between 1930 and 1960, certain fundamentalist groups underwent a change in their thinking. Members became more informed and a little less frightened by mainline Protestant theology. This period also saw the rise and expansion of the fundamentalist "nondenominational denominations." A fundamentalist subculture gradually developed with its gospel songs, Bible colleges, radio programs and the like.

Whereas the first generation of fundamentalists avoided the world, waiting eagerly for Jesus' Second Coming and his destruction of the world, the second generation of fundamentalists began gradually to seek out recognition by the world. As a result, fundamentalism gradually developed a permanent belief system and theology.

3) Third phase: 'embrace' of the media and America

This third phase of fundamentalism is characterized by the capture of the media which began about 1960 and has continued into the present day. One thinks of the rise of such media superstars as Oral Roberts, Rex Humbard and Billy Graham.

It is ironic that a group of people, one of whose principal tenets is that the world is evil and to be avoided, has become highly skilled at using the world's own devices to propagate its message. It is paradoxical that a group which fears and mistrusts science has succeeded largely because of its use of modern technology. (This is not to criticize the fundamentalists. In fact, Catholics could certainly learn something from fundamentalists in this area. There is not a single Catholic television program which achieves anything like the significance of, for example, the *700 Club*.)

Fundamentalism in this third phase of its 20th-century

life (1960 to the present) has entered the political process through such groups as the Moral Majority. Instead of shrinking from contact with the world while it awaits the final cataclysm, certain fundamentalists today actively seek to influence the world's structures. Latter-day fundamentalism has adapted itself to and wholeheartedly endorses everything American. God, country, flag, technology and money-making are now all interwoven in the fabric of certain fundamentalist theology.

Common Fundamentalist Tendencies

Despite a wide variation from one group to another, we can define the following general tendencies within fundamentalism. What I will define is just that—*tendencies*. I do not suggest that *all* fundamentalists exhibit *all* of these characteristics.

1) Legalism

Although fundamentalists constantly reiterate their belief in salvation by faith and not by law, the essential characteristic of fundamentalism is its *legalism*. By legalism I mean a literal or excessive conformity to a religious or moral code for its own sake.

Fundamentalists take a legalistic approach to every question by making the Bible the ultimate authority. The Bible is used by fundamentalists much like a lawbook. Underlying this legalistic approach to the Bible is the belief that God speaks to humanity directly in the Bible—that is, that God dictated to the writers of the Bible the very words he wanted written.

For fundamentalists the Bible is thus absolutely unerring in every single detail, even in those details of science, geography and cosmology which we know to be incorrect. We will discuss this question of biblical inerrancy further in Chapter Two.

The fundamentalists' use of the Bible almost as a law code leads to a legalistic theology. There is a certain body of accepted beliefs to which one must adhere, according to the fundamentalist, or else one is not a Christian. Paradoxically, many of these fundamentalist doctrines are not found in Scripture, at least not in the form that fundamentalists teach them.

For example, nowhere in the Bible does it say that you must accept Jesus as "your personal Lord and Savior." (I don't

14

deny the validity of the statement, but the way fundamentalists misuse it.) Nor is one of today's favorite fundamentalist buzzwords, "the Rapture," mentioned anywhere in the Bible. Nor does the Bible say that Scripture is the "infallible Word of God." (As we shall see later, the Bible really says all Scripture is *inspired* by God.)

Further, none of these slogans as applied by the fundamentalists really conveys the concerns of the early Church. They have been invented by fundamentalists only in the last two centuries. Despite this fact, fundamentalist theology proclaims that its beliefs, and its beliefs alone, constitute normative Christianity.

Fundamentalism's legalistic theology translates into the legalistic life-style which fundamentalism promotes. After having lived among fundamentalist groups from time to time, and after having lived many years in the South, my experience has been that there is little originality or creativity among fundamentalists.

The rite of initiation into fundamentalist life is the altar call, a legalistic type of public proclamation of one's belief in the fundamentalist credo. (It is similar to the loyalty oath one takes to become a citizen.) Let us contrast this fundamentalist invention (there is no "altar call" mentioned in the Bible) with the early Church's rite of initiation.

The early Church required a lengthy period of instruction called the *catechumenate* before it administered the Sacrament of Baptism, which the Church always regarded as a great mystery rather than as a legal proclamation of one's public standing. Fundamentalism strips Christianity of its mystery and replaces it with legalistic certainty. As a result, fundamentalist life is reduced to a list of "do's and don'ts" and Christianity becomes not a call to freedom (as intended) but a set of rules to be kept. (I freely acknowledge that we Catholics have been guilty of this same mentality. So were the Pharisees.)

Fundamentalist life is a great quest for individual sanctity; it places all the focus on one's own personal holiness. As a result, fundamentalists are unconcerned about the complexities of sin and evil—particularly the *social dimension* of injustice. All problems are solvable by the proper answer to the question, "Have *you* been saved?"

Fundamentalist ethics are involved with a long list of

trivialities. Such things as card-playing, drinking alcoholic beverages, attendance at movies, dancing and reading certain proscribed books are all condemned as anti-Christian. Fundamentalist ethics are thus oriented toward personal purity and ignore the underlying *causes* of evil in social injustice and materialistic greed.

One reason for this legalistic ethos is that fundamentalists really refuse to let Jesus (and thus every other human being) be human. Fundamentalists are, in a sense, *docetists*—from the Greek word for "to seem." (Docetism was a prominent second-century Gnostic heresy which held that Jesus only *seemed* to be human.)

Fundamentalists appear unable to believe that Jesus was really like the rest of us mortals. As a trivial example—greatly magnified by fundamentalists—they insist that Jesus used grape juice at the Last Supper. They can't imagine that Jesus drank wine, even though it was undisputedly the staple beverage for Jews of Jesus' day. Likewise, fundamentalists often seem unable to believe that Jesus really loved sinners or that he really wanted to associate with them. For fundamentalists, sinners are "souls" to be won. Jesus, on the other hand, came to save not just souls, but persons, and freely associated in every respect with them.

During the 1980 Cuban refugee crisis in Florida, a television interviewer asked a fundamentalist preacher his perspective on the problem. He replied, "Well, what I would do would be to save them all and then send them back to Cuba." Fundamentalists apparently see Jesus as someone who goes around holding his nose while associating with filthy sinners simply so that he can save their souls. The Bible reveals quite the opposite picture—that Jesus really does love sinners and that he really does enter into their lives as human beings in a fully human way.

Fundamentalists also tend to reify—make a *thing* of—Jesus, grace and God's will. This is illustrated in one of the favorite fundamentalist refrains: "I pray that you'll *find* Jesus."

In actuality we don't "find" Jesus. Jesus finds *us*. He comes to us in our actual lives as human beings. Ironically, in placing the emphasis the other way around, fundamentalists deny the biblical way of looking at life.

The Jews of Old and New Testament times would not have had the slightest idea what was meant by a question such as, "Have you found God?" or, "Have you accepted God?" God had found *them*, and they experienced God in their lives through their own human experiences. Rather than looking upon God as something separate to be "found" (and possessed), the Hebrews knew God as someone who came to them in an intimate relationship and who revealed himself by acting in their human history.

Fundamentalism also sees grace as an "it" rather than as an event or a moment of *relationship* which God initiates. This perspective leads to the fundamentalist belief in the one single moment of salvation: Once one has received "grace"—the big "it"—one has irrevocably been "saved."

Likewise, to fundamentalists, God's will is an "it" to be "found." In actuality, God's will is our own will submitted to God's plan for us as revealed in Scripture and the Church's shared life as the Body of Christ.

Neither life, Jesus, grace nor God's will are quantifiable *things* reducible to formulas or capable of possession. Life, Jesus, grace and God's will are all beyond our power to comprehend. They are not—as some fundamentalists tend to make them—elements in an algebraic equation. God is ultimately mystery, and if we reduce God to "the known" we have simply made him over into our own image and likeness.

This is precisely the teaching of the Old Testament Book of Job. Job's friends—good fundamentalists—thought they had God all figured out. Job came to realize that God is much greater than anything his fundamentalist friends said.

2) Ignorance of history

One morning when I was about 11 years old, I was listening to my mother and a fundamentalist woman on our front porch discuss their differing religious views. After a good half hour of argument, our visitor stamped her feet, slammed down her Bible, looked at my mother and said, "Well, I just have one more thing to say to you: If the *King James Version* of the Bible was good enough for St. Paul, it's good enough for me."

This story is my favorite illustration of the great ignorance on the part of many fundamentalists concerning the historical development of both the Bible and the Church. Another is the fundamentalist denomination which claims in its billboards to have been "founded by Jesus Christ in 33 A.D." (This denomination, in fact, traces its origin to a man named Alexander Campbell who lived in the 19th century.)

Fundamentalists often ignore history. They overlook the fact that the Christian Church and the Bible originated in certain very specific historical settings and were shaped by certain very specific historical forces.

For example, fundamentalists claim to be "pure Bible Churches," meaning that they somehow exist isolated from all historical conditioning in a world exactly like that depicted in the New Testament. In reality, there never was any such thing as a "pure Bible Church."

Do the fundamentalists suppose that St. Paul carried a leather book engraved "Holy Bible" with him on his missionary journeys or that he read "Paul's Epistles" to his audiences? The early Church existed for two centuries before it came to even a tentative consensus as to which books were to be placed in the New Testament. The early Church based its life not only on its gradually developing biblical literature, but on the oral teaching of the apostles and other elders, as well as on other revered writings.

Out of this picture of early Church life certain undisputed historical facts emerge. By the early second century the Church was forming its episcopal character. And by the early third century it was definitely fixed as an episcopal Church, that is, a Church led by bishops.

Further, the sacraments of Baptism and Eucharist were indispensable elements of the life of the early Church. To strip these sacraments from Christianity today—as some fundamentalist groups do—is essentially to deny Christianity two of its foundational elements.

Finally, the *full* understanding which the early Church had of itself is not found simply in the New Testament. One has to look as well to the great creedal formulas worked out beginning in the second century and culminating in the fourth and fifth centuries. These creeds, like the Bible itself, grew out of and were conditioned by historical forces to which the Church responded. Throughout the centuries historical forces have continued to play a large part in shaping the Church as we know it today.

One cannot, therefore, ignore 2,000 years of God's work in history and leap back presumptuously to "33 A.D.," as some fundamentalists attempt to do. Unless one is somehow connected with Christianity as it has *developed* from its first beginnings, one is out of touch with the real Christianity. The "true" Church is the Church that has actually evolved through history from its primitive origins in New Testament times to today.

3) Individualism

The focus in fundamentalism is on one's personal—that is, *individual*—salvation and right-standing before God. Fundamentalist piety, worship and theology are *I*-centered rather than *we*-centered. The New Testament, on the other hand, reveals that salvation is for the collective People of God, the Church. Certainly the New Testament does not ignore one's responsibility for one's own salvation. Yet its ultimate emphasis is on God's *people*, not on the individual.

Jesus chose 12 companions to accompany him in his mission. He spoke often of a Kingdom—a corporate, communal concept. The word *Christ* itself is identified specifically with the Church (Ephesians 4:15-16; 5:29-33). God's plan as revealed in Scripture included "us" (Hebrews 11:40), not "me": Through *us* salvation spreads to others. The early Church as depicted in Acts 4:32 is very obviously not an I-centered Church. And, finally, the sacraments established by Jesus were intended to be aids for *communal* life (see 1 Corinthians 10:16).

In contrast to the communal thrust of the New Testament, many fundamentalists assume that Christ and the Church are somehow distinct. Their concern is that someone "comes to Christ" rather than that someone comes to Christ *through the Church*. Yet one cannot fully come to Christ without coming into his Church at the same time. Incorporation into Christ means precisely incorporation into his earthly Body, the Church.

Once someone is "saved" at a football stadium altar call or "gives herself to Christ" by touching a television screen at the invitation of a TV evangelist, where does that leave the person? The great danger of fundamentalist mass evangelism is that it gives people the false understanding that they are incorporated into the Body of Christ simply because they have "accepted" or "found" Jesus. I don't deny that "accepting Jesus as one's personal savior" at a rally or altar call may be for some people a *starting point* for conversion, but such an experience by itself is not, as fundamentalists tend to make it, the whole cloth of Christianity.

Fundamentalism's individualistic thrust is exemplified in its worship, which sometimes resembles a one-man show. (We Catholics remember the pre-Vatican II days when the priest had his back turned to the congregation and all attention was focused on the man at the altar. This too was a distortion of true Christian worship.) Christian worship, at its heart, is participation, not entertainment. Many fundamentalist Churches stress the entertainment value of worship in church buildings consciously mimicking the architectural style of theaters. These structures—like fundamentalist theology—are oriented toward words and talk rather than toward mystery, which lies at the very heart of Christian worship.

Fundamentalist individualism is also revealed in the catch words and phrases of its fellowship: "*I* know the Lord," "The Lord spoke to *me*," "Jesus is my *personal* savior." None of these fundamentalist slogans appear in the New Testament. And, if asserted to their logical conclusion, they contradict both the communal spirit which permeates the New Testament and the New Testament belief in communal discernment of individual revelation (see 1 John 4:1-6). What the Lord tells *me* must ultimately be judged by the shared discernment of the entire body of believers of which I am but one member.

The New Testament portrays the Church as a pilgrim people constantly on the move, building up the Kingdom of God in ever new and changing circumstances. The New Testament does not depict the Church as a loose collection of "saved" individuals for whom the battle is all over—which is the image one frequently gets in listening to fundamentalists.

4) Negative attitude toward creation

Many fundamentalists' abhorrence of modern science shows that they are uncomfortable with the ever-deepening understanding of God's creation which science gives us.

Fundamentalists are inclined to focus more intently on God's redemption than on his continuing work as Creator. They tend to separate God's redemption from his act of creation. In reality God both creates and redeems humanity (and all creation) through his constant presence in creation.

Fundamentalists are often so concerned with techniques

20

of salvation that they consider God himself interested only in religion. Yet in reality God is concerned not with religion, but with his *creation*—the people and things he has brought and continues to bring into being.

I remember a conversation I had with a fundamentalist lady who accused us Catholics of being too "humanistic." The more I pursued her remark the more I realized that what she really meant was that Catholics don't believe sufficiently in humanity's badness. This fundamentalist suspicion of God's creation stems from a false understanding of Jesus' sacrifice on the cross and of the doctrine of the atonement.

A fundamentalist friend recently took me to a large gathering where a famous fundamentalist preacher was holding forth on this topic. The preacher compared Abraham's near-sacrifice of his son Isaac to God's actual sacrifice of Jesus, with the difference that, as he put it, when it came time for Jesus to die, "God killed him."

This attitude lies at the heart of the fundamentalist doctrine of the "substitutionary atonement." Fundamentalists view God as taking out his anger against the human race on Jesus instead of punishing wicked us. In actuality, *God* did not kill Jesus; evil *people* killed Jesus. Jesus freely gave his life up as a love offering for others. He was not pushed into it by a despotic divine Father who wanted to avenge his wrath against sinful humanity.

This misconception of the atonement lies at the root of the generally negative fundamentalist attitude toward creation and likewise explains why there is no fundamentalist art, literature, music or culture of any consequence. There can be no real culture among people who believe that humanity is horrid in God's eyes. The great works of Christian culture come from the hands of Christians—such as Michelangelo or Bach—who believe in the essential goodness of redeemed humanity.

5) Relationship with 'the world'

As we look at the world around us we see the popular acceptance of abortion, breakdown of family values, media debasement of culture, an ever-growing nuclear arms race, an increase in sexual immorality, greed and materialism on a mass scale, loss of privacy and individual autonomy, great social injustice present everywhere in the world, widespread poverty and hunger, and many other evils. All these evils can tempt us to throw up our hands and leave the wickedness of the world to God's vengeful judgment—the position taken by many fundamentalists.

This is precisely why fundamentalism is so appealing today. It offers quick and easy solutions to all of life's insecurities and uncertainties. Simply "be saved," "accept Jesus" and then wait for Jesus to come and punish all the sinners who are causing these great evils.

The sordid state of the world today is due largely to the fact that many Christians have accepted a false understanding of their relationship with the world: the illusion that Christianity should entirely segregate itself from the world and focus instead only on doctrine and religion. In reality the Church and the world are inextricably bound up together. The very focal point of the Church's mission is—like it or not—the oftentimes depressing world around us.

To the extent that fundamentalists remind us that the Church must not be *like* the world, however, they have a valid lesson to teach. We must be "*in* the world but not *of* the world" (see John 17:14-18). We must be radically different from the world as we seek to transform it into the Kingdom of God.

Many Christians today have become so perplexed by the problems of the world that they try to solve these problems solely through the world's methods. Fundamentalists can serve to remind us, for example, that the Church should not become just another social welfare organization or charitable institution, but must offer instead a solution which is radically different from the world's materialistic value system. The difference between fundamentalists and Catholics on this point is that the former tend to take a "hands-off" approach when it comes to using the world's methods, while Catholicism attempts to integrate these methods into the teaching of the gospel.

Catholicism maintains that nothing God has created is bad in itself. Even further, nothing that humanity has developed to *explain* God's creation—psychology, sociology or science, for example—are evils to be avoided simply because they have in some circumstances led to the establishment of unchristian values in the modern world. Instead of opposing these disciplines, as fundamentalists often do, Christians should instead seek to enter fully into such disciplines, find what is potentially good in them and then incorporate that good into the message of the gospel.

Fundamentalism's Good Points

Do I see any good in fundamentalism? I do. I think we can identify the following good points and that these can serve as elements around which Catholics can develop a true dialogue with those fundamentalists open to it.

1) The desire to base one's life on God's revelation in the Bible

This fundamentalist desire lies at the core of Christianity. Even though—as we shall see in the next chapter—Catholics and fundamentalists disagree on how to approach the Bible, Catholics are by and large seriously negligent in Bible study and reading. Fortunately, however, many Catholics today are rediscovering the Bible, and in this lies a hopeful sign for a rapprochement with some fundamentalists.

2) The quest for personal holiness

This fundamentalist quest is an important aspect of Christian life. Although fundamentalists may overexaggerate the immorality of many actions which are not inherently evil, Catholics nevertheless should realize that many of the fundamentalist taboos do point out the possibility for sin. For example, drinking alcoholic beverages is not an evil in itself, but it certainly can become an evil if it is abused. Some fundamentalist suspicion of the world's enticements is certainly not without foundation.

3) The necessity for making clear-cut and obvious moral choices

Fundamentalists certainly put their money where their mouth is in this respect. They truly try to live what they preach while, sadly, many other Christians often seem to have a very shifting, tenuous morality.

4) The desire to find and restore absolute standards in a world of confusing relativities

This is something that we all can appreciate in this day

and age. Perhaps modern Catholicism has been guilty at times of going to the other extreme by practicing "situation ethics"—that is, by proclaiming a morality which too easily says, "It all depends." There *is* sin in the world, and we should denounce sin for what it is rather than try to explain it away.

We Catholics should listen to the claims of moderate and informed fundamentalists in these four areas in order to see where we have room for improvement.

No working definition of fundamentalism would be complete without discussing how fundamentalists view the Bible. The next chapter contrasts the Catholic and fundamentalist approaches to sacred Scripture.

CHAPTER TWO

Who's Right About the Bible?

A fundamentalist minister recently told me about a woman who had parked her car in the center of the only two parking spaces on a crowded city street. He related how he had approached the woman and, during the course of their "discussion," had become angry and called her a rather vulgar name.

I interrupted him to ask if this was consistent with Jesus' instruction to "turn the other cheek" (see Matthew 5:39). The preacher replied that Jesus had said to turn the other cheek only when one had first been struck on the cheek. I asked him if he understood Jesus' words to mean that if I struck someone angrily on the *shoulder* the person would not be enjoined to turn the other shoulder. The man's reply was, "Of course not!"

In other words, this fundamentalist preacher saw Jesus' words as being concerned solely with that area surrounding the facial bones which we call the cheek. Jesus, in this man's estimation, was not the least bit concerned with the underlying causes of violence, aggression and anger. This experience demonstrates how difficult it can be to discuss the Bible with fundamentalists.

Noted Catholic Scripture scholar Father Eugene Laverdiere has observed that fundamentalism is not a particular interpretation of the Bible, but the lack of any interpretation. Fundamentalists accept the words of Scripture at face value, literally.

Sadly, because of this prevalent fundamentalist approach to Scripture, it is impossible to communicate with some fundamentalists concerning the meaning of God's revelation in the Bible. Many fundamentalists seem unable to read the Bible in the context intended by its authors because they believe it was dictated by God directly to the human authors of Scripture. Because of their lack of historical perspective concerning the *development* of the Bible, they cannot understand that the Bible is God's Word given to us through centuries of historical and cultural conditioning.

I remember once having an argument with a fundamentalist who constantly kept asking me, "Would you like to know what Scripture has to say about that?" After allowing him several times to read unrelated and irrelevant Scripture passages to me, I finally told him, "No, I do not want to know what Scripture *says* about that. I want to know what Scripture *means* about that."

As I discovered during my discussion with this man, it is pointless to enter into a game of scriptural badminton with fundamentalists—to quote Scripture passages back and forth, trying to accumulate more points than one's opponent. The problem with this type of discussion is that frequently a difference exists between what Scripture "says" and what it "means."

The words of Scripture were written by people whose perspectives were much different than ours. They lived in different surroundings; their styles of thinking and speaking were much different than ours. To impose our 20th-century mentality on the words they used is very often to distort those words. We must constantly seek to enter into the perspective of the authors themselves, rather than assume that the authors intended—millennia ago!—to speak as 20th-century Americans.

That is why biblical scholarship is so important. Scripture scholars help us to see that the Bible arose in a world vastly different from our own, where people thought very differently than we do, and where writing was done in many different literary genres—some of which are no longer used by writers today.

Scriptural scholarship also challenges our idea of the Bible as a "book." The Bible is not *a* book but *many* books brought into a unified form over many centuries—and after much struggle and disagreement among many people as to which books should be included and which excluded from the finished product. (We will discuss later in this chapter how the various versions and translations of the Bible came into existence.)

To illustrate the fallacy of the fundamentalist understanding of the Bible as a single book coming into existence in whole cloth, all at once, as well as the fallacy of trying to read the books of the Bible from our own perspective, let's imagine the following two occurrences.

Suppose that an archaeologist probing through the remains of our civilization 2,000 years from now discovers fragments of newspapers, textbooks, novels, short stories and personal diaries. If the archaeologist read each one of the discovered fragments from the perspective of the year 3984, and did not understand—as we do—that each type of literature was intended for different audiences and purposes, serious errors would creep into his or her conclusions about our civilization. If, further, those fragments of different types of literature were bound together into one volume and read straight through from beginning to end, the reader—2,000 years from now—would be hopelessly confused as to the point of the "book." Unfortunately, many fundamentalists today are similarly confused and mistaken in many of their conclusions concerning the purpose and the meaning of the Bible.

A second illustration is borrowed from Dr. George Martin's *Reading Scripture as the Word of God.* Dr. Martin hypothesizes an archaeologist coming across fragments of newspapers 2,000 years after they have been printed. The bold print reads, "Lions Clobber Bears," "Rams Upended by Redskins," "Pirates Slaughter Yankees, Capture Series." If that archaeologist knows nothing about our society other than what is in those fragments, he or she—once again—will grossly distort the meaning and the purpose of the literature discovered.

The difference between Catholics and fundamentalists as to the meaning or purpose of Scripture comes down to this basic issue: How are we to understand God's *inspiration* of the Bible, on the one hand, and the *inerrancy* (or infallibility) of the text on the other? Catholics and fundamentalists mean something different when they say that the Bible is "inspired by God." Further, they mean something different when they say that Scripture is "inerrant." (Note that both Catholics and fundamentalists do use the same terms.) In order to understand this difference between the Catholic and fundamentalist positions on inspiration and inerrancy, let us take a look at these two concepts.

'Inspiration' and 'Inerrancy': The Catholic View

Let's first look at the Catholic understanding of the inspiration of Scripture. The Bible itself refers to the concept of inspiration in 2 Timothy 3:16, where the writer says, "All Scripture is *inspired of God* and is useful for teaching—for reproof, correction and training in holiness" (emphasis added). The Greek word used in this passage for "inspired of God" is *theopneustos*, which literally means "God-breathed." (Incidentally, when the writer says "all Scripture," he is referring to the Old Testament since, at the time he wrote, the New Testament was not in existence.)

Interestingly, the ancient Israelites had no notion of the inspired quality of the words of their sacred Scriptures. They believed that God inspired the prophets to *act* and *speak*, but they did not believe that the actual written words in their Scriptures were "God-breathed" or (as in 2 Peter 1:21) that the writers were "impelled by the Holy Spirit."

By Jesus' time the Jews had come to see the written words themselves as, in some sense, inspired by God. Over centuries of reflection on their sacred literature the Jews had gradually developed a concept of inspiration. One of their leading historians, Josephus, who wrote roughly during the time of Jesus, commented on this Jewish belief:

> It is an instinct with every Jew from the day of his birth, to regard the sacred Scriptures as the decrees of God, to abide by them, and, if necessary, to die for them gladly.

It was this Jewish reverence for the words of Scripture as "the decrees of God" which is expressed in 2 Timothy 3:16. The Jewish reverence was accepted by the writers of the New Testament (most of whom were Jews). In John's Gospel, for example, we find Jesus saying, "...Scripture cannot lose its force" (10:35). In Matthew's Gospel Jesus says three times, in response to the devil's temptation, "Scripture has it..." (4:4,7,10)—a phrase he repeats on the eve of Good Friday (Matthew 26:31). When the Pharisees question him about divorce, Jesus responds, "Have you not read...?" (Matthew 19:4-5).

From the examples of the primitive *kerygma* (or early proclamation of the gospel) recorded in the Acts of the Apostles we likewise see this emphasis by the early Church on Scripture as the inspired Word of God. In Acts 1:16 Peter refers to a saying in Scripture "uttered long ago *by the Holy Spirit* through the mouth of David" (emphasis added).

Paul likewise shares this early Christian belief. He says in Romans 9:17, "*Scripture* says to Pharaoh...." If we turn to the scene which Paul had in mind (Exodus 9:16), we find that in reality it is Yahweh himself who is speaking. Thus Paul equates "Scripture" with the very words of Yahweh himself. (For a similar example, see Galatians 3:8 and Genesis 12:3).

The New Testament writers' belief in the inspired quality of Scripture was continued by the early Church fathers. For example, Clement of Alexandria (150-215) called God the "author" of Scripture. One of the first great Catholic Scripture scholars, St. Jerome (342-420), said that God was the "one author" of the many Epistles of St. Paul. (This belief that Paul's letters were also inspired by God appears in the New Testament itself: See 2 Peter 3:15-16, where Paul's letters are compared to "the rest of Scripture.")

Pope Gregory I, "the Great" (540-604), referred to God as the "author" of Scripture. The greatest doctor of the medieval Catholic Church, Thomas Aquinas (1225-1274), called God the "principal author of Scripture." Finally, in our own day the bishops of the Catholic Church affirmed this consistent Catholic belief in the inspiration of the Bible:

> ...[T]he books of the Old and New Testment, whole and entire, with all their parts [were] written under the inspiration of the Holy Spirit, and as such they have God as their author and have been handed on as such to the Church herself.
> (*Dogmatic Constitution on Divine Revelation*, #11)

We see then that understanding Scripture as God's Word is very much a part of the Catholic tradition and has consistently been taught by the Church as a constituent element of its doctrine.

The Word of God in human words

Thus far fundamentalists would perhaps be in substantial agreement with the Catholic understanding of inspiration. There is another element, however, which often divides Catholics and fundamentalists: the Catholic understanding of God's Word as mediated to us in and through human authors.

This "humanness" of Scripture was understood by the Jews themselves well before the time of Jesus. For example, in the Book of Sirach (Ecclesiasticus)—one of the Greek books not in the Protestant Bible—the writer says in his Foreword:

> You therefore are now invited to read [the following passages] in a spirit of attentive good will, with indulgence for any apparent failure on our part, despite earnest efforts, in the interpretation of particular passages. For words spoken originally in Hebrew are not as effective when they are translated into another language. That is true not only of this book but of the law itself, the prophets and the rest of the books, which differ no little when they are read in the original.

Another of the Old Testament writers expresses this same sense of his human involvement in writing God's words when he says,

> For us who have taken upon ourselves the labor of making this digest, the task, far from being easy, is one of sweat and of sleepless nights, just as the preparation of a festive banquet is no light matter for one who thus seeks to give enjoyment to others....If it is well written and to the point, that is what I wanted; if it is poorly done and mediocre, that is the best I could do.
>
> (2 Maccabees 2:26-27; 15:38)

Neither Sirach nor 2 Maccabees is accepted by fundamentalists as inspired Scripture, but the point is made nonetheless that the writers of ancient Jewish Scripture freely expressed their human foibles in taking up their tasks. (We will consider later in this chapter the question of the difference between the Protestant and the Catholic versions of the Old Testament.)

This sense of God's Word coming to us in the words of human authors is expressed in the New Testament as well. For example, in the preface to Luke's Gospel we read,

> Many have undertaken to compile a narrative of the events which have been fulfilled in our midst, precisely as those events were transmitted to us by the original eyewitnesses and ministers of the word.
>
> (Luke 1:1-2)

Luke is telling us that the Gospel he is about to write was not dictated to him by God from heaven, but that it came to him in large measure from his discussions with "original eyewitnesses and ministers of the word."

Paul likewise gives us an example of the humanness of God's Word. In 1 Corinthians 1:14-16 he says,

> Thank God, I baptized none of you except Crispus and Gaius, so there are none who can say that you were baptized in my name. Oh, and I baptized the household of Stephanas. Beyond that, I am not aware of having baptized anyone else.

If we accept the fundamentalist position that God dictated to Paul the very words which God wanted in the Bible, we would have to conclude that God momentarily forgot that Paul had baptized the household of Stephanas. In reality, what we see in this passage is yet another example of how the writer's humanity pervades and underlies God's *own* Word in Scripture.

Just as the early Church fathers emphasized God's inspiration of Scripture, so too they emphasized this human element. For example, the leading scholar and most prolific writer of the early Church, Origen of Alexandria (185-254), frequently emphasized that the writers of sacred Scripture did not lose their free will when they wrote but used their own human faculties.

St. Augustine (354-430), like Origen, emphasized that the Gospel writers relied upon their own human memories and faculties in composing their writings. Thomas Aquinas, who as we have seen, called God the "principal author of Scripture" referred at the same time to the human "instrumental author." Finally, the bishops at Vatican II likewise spoke of this union between divine inspiration and human participation:

> Seeing that, in sacred Scripture, God speaks through men in human fashion, it follows that the interpreter of sacred Scriptures, if he is to ascertain what God has wished to communicate to us, should carefully search out the meaning which the sacred writers had in mind, that meaning that God had thought well to manifest through the medium of their words.... Rightly to understand what the sacred author wanted to affirm in his work, due attention must be paid both to the customary and characteristic patterns of perception, speech and narrative which prevailed at the age of the sacred writer, and to the conventions which the people of his time followed in their dealings with one another....Indeed the words of God, expressed in the words of men, are in every way like human language, just as the Word of the eternal Father, when he took on himself the flesh of human weakness, became like men.
>
> (*Dogmatic Constitution on Divine Revelation*, #12, 13)

Earlier I referred to fundamentalists as being docetic (see p. 16). This is exemplified no more clearly than in their approach to the Bible. Whereas the bishops at Vatican II remind us that Jesus really took on the "flesh of human weakness" and, by analogy, that the Word of God really comes to us in the words of human beings, fundamentalists want to place both Jesus and the words of Scripture on a pedestal far removed from their actual humanity. In their perspective, Jesus and the Bible only *appear* to be human. The Catholic position, on the other hand, is that Jesus and the Bible are both fully human and divine.

The Bible's diverse sources
Another way to illustrate the Bible's humanness is to

discuss the different perspectives or sources from which the Bible was written. One of the earliest examples of this in the Bible is found in Exodus 14:15-26—the scene of the Israelites' escape from Pharaoh.

First we read that "the LORD swept the sea with a strong east wind throughout the night and so turned it into dry land" (14:21). At this point, then, the Red Sea has been blown dry by the Lord and it is now dry land. Yet in the very next sentence we read, "When the water was thus divided, the Israelites marched into the midst of the sea on dry land, with the water like a wall to their right and to their left" (14:21-22). What happened to the "dry land" we just left?

Here two different sources, or two different perspectives on the Israelites' escape from Egypt and their passage through the Red Sea, have been united. One source remembers the escape from Pharaoh as a walk through a shallow marshy area that had been dried up by God through a mighty wind. Another source or perspective remembered the event much differently—as a Cecil B. DeMille march between walls of water. God's revelation to the human authors of this portion of Exodus, then, comes down to us through two different traditions.

Another example of two differing perspectives appearing side by side in Scripture occurs in the Book of Genesis. We read that, before God created humanity, "…as yet there was no field shrub on earth and no grass of the field had sprouted…" (2:5). Yet Genesis 1:1-31 conveys just the opposite impression—that God created all the other elements of nature *before* he created us. Once again, we see two different traditions at work in the writing of Scripture, each one bringing us a different perspective on the same event.

This difference in perspective is also evident in the New Testament. For example, compare Matthew's version of Jesus' discourse on the Beatitudes (5:1-12) with Luke's (6:17-26). Matthew places Jesus on a mountainside, where he gathers his disciples around him before beginning what is obviously a very formal address. His words are directed not to people in intimate contact with him, but rather to people who are characterized according to certain descriptions: "the poor in spirit," the "sorrowing," "the lowly."

Further, Matthew's Jesus is concerned with such concepts as *spiritual* poverty and the people's hunger and thirst for *holiness*. We could say that Matthew's perspective on Jesus' discourse is *"future-oriented,"* seeing the people as they will become once the Kingdom of God has reached its fullness.

Luke takes a much different approach. Jesus is not on a mountain, but on a "level stretch." Luke's Jesus does not "stage" the event so as to emphasize its solemnity; rather, he is simply walking along on the level stretch, curing the people's illnesses when, all of a sudden, he breaks into a discourse on the Beatitudes.

Notice that for Luke's Jesus the poor are not categorized as types but as actual people in close proximity to Jesus. He does not refer to *"the* poor," but rather to *"you* poor," and *"you* who hunger" and *"you* who are weeping." Further, Luke adds four "woes" (6:24-26). Luke's Jesus concretizes his remarks in the *here and now*.

Luke warns his readers against pursuing wealth, full stomachs and power in the world. He emphasizes that the Kingdom of God is a practical and material reality in the lives of believers, while Matthew emphasizes the Kingdom's spiritual dimensions.

Thus in the New Testament as in the Old the human authors of God's revealed Word are very much involved through their own personalities, perspectives and points of view. The four Gospels abound with examples such as the one we have just seen. We can simply conclude, as the bishops at Vatican II have concluded, that God's Word is revealed to us in the words of human beings who share our humanity fully—with all of its foibles, biases and weaknesses as well as all of its intelligence, creativity and insight.

That is the Catholic view of inspiration and inerrancy. Now, what is the fundamentalist view?

'Inspiration' and 'Inerrancy': The Fundamentalist View

For fundamentalists the words of the Bible themselves—at their face value—were divinely revealed to the writers of the Bible and must be accepted—solely on their face value—as divine truth. For fundamentalists there is no probing beneath the words; thus, fundamentalists reject scholarly findings which emphasize the human contribution to the books.

This fundamentalist approach leads to great problems. For example, what does one do about manifest inconsistencies in the text? For instance, Mark 15:25 says, "It was about nine in the morning when they crucified him." John 19:14, on the other hand, states that at *noon* on the day of his crucifixion Jesus was still standing before Pilate on the stone pavement called Gabbatha. When was Jesus crucified—at nine in the morning or sometime in the afternoon? If one takes the fundamentalist approach to Scripture, one must conclude that God had a momentary lapse of memory when he was dictating this particular scene.

Then there is the problem of taking the Bible literally. How "literal" is literal? To illustrate the dimensions of this problem, look at Luke 14:12-13: "*Whenever* you give a lunch or dinner, do not invite your friends or brothers or relatives or wealthy neighbors. They might invite you in return and thus repay you. No, when you have a reception, invite beggars and the crippled, the lame and the blind" (emphasis added).

Do fundamentalists *never* give a lunch or dinner to which they have invited their friends or brothers, their relatives or their wealthy neighbors? I recall attending family reunions of fundamentalist friends and seeing "friends, brothers, relatives and wealthy neighbors" in abundance. I saw no beggars there, nor lame or blind persons. Were those fundamentalists ignoring God's "direct command" in Scripture?

These two illustrations demonstrate the futility of the fundamentalist approach to the Bible. Fundamentalists take an all-or-nothing approach to Scripture, and must expend great amounts of mental energy defending this approach. As a result, they are constantly on guard to fend off the slightest challenge. This attitude lies at the root of much of the paranoia and insecurity one encounters when harangued by a "Bible-quoting" fundamentalist.

As a corollary to their view of Scripture, fundamentalists are forced to presume that not only were the *authors* of the original Hebrew and Greek manuscripts inspired by God, but the *translators* of these manuscripts were likewise inspired. For fundamentalists base their perspective on inerrancy solely on the *English* words, rather than on the original Hebrew and Greek. In reality the translators of the original manuscripts were *not* inspired, at least, not to the same degree as the original authors.

In the face of this distinction between the English versions and the ancient originals, fundamentalists insist that there is one and only one English version which represents the inspired translation of the original manuscripts: The *King James Version*. In fact, we could define an "orthodox" fundamentalist today as someone who insists that the *King James Version* is the only accurate and authentic translation of the original Hebrew and Greek manuscripts. (There are many Protestants who *use* the *King James Version* but who do accept other versions as accurate renditions of the original manuscripts into English.)

In the South I see this fundamentalist insistence on the *King James Version* emphasized frequently today. Many fundamentalists have bumper stickers on their cars which read, "The *KJV* is God's Word!" These fundamentalists must assume that the 16th-century English scholars who prepared the *King James Version* somehow expressed the ancient Hebrew and Greek words in 20th-century English.

Like everything else concerning the Bible, fundamentalists are not open to probing questions and dialogue on this issue of translations of the Bible, and thus it is very difficult to communicate with them. Unless a person uses "ye" and "thou" and "wouldst" in quoting Scripture to a fundamentalist, that person is likely to be charged with using one of the "devil-inspired" modern versions of the Bible.

In order to be able to respond adequately to this fundamentalist insistence on the *King James Version* as the only acceptable English rendering of the ancient manuscripts, we must say something about how the English Bible evolved into its present form.

How We Got Today's Bible

The very first Hebrew Bible was nothing like a book as we know books today. Rather, it was a set of written scrolls which, collectively, came to be known as the Bible (from the Greek *byblos*, "book"). This Hebrew Bible was translated first into Greek and then into Latin (among other languages). The *first* scrolls—which were written in Hebrew—have been lost for centuries; *copies* of these scrolls, as well as their Greek and Latin translations, have been the only documents at scholars' disposal for hundreds of years.

Interestingly, today's scholars actually have more ancient sources to work from than were available to the 16th-century translators of the *King James Version*. Historical and archaeological discoveries since the 16th century have uncovered many original materials which were not available to the translators of the first English Bibles.

The most famous ancient manuscripts recently discovered are the Dead Sea Scrolls, ancient Jewish writings unearthed in 1947 and subsequent years in isolated Palestinian caves. One segment of these scrolls, called the Qumran manuscripts (after the area in Palestine where the caves are located), has been particularly helpful to present-day Bible scholars: Portions of the Qumran manuscripts include scrolls from the Hebrew Bible which are hundreds of years older than scrolls previously known.

Scholars are thus able to compare the Qumran manuscripts with the *younger* manuscripts available to the 16th-century translators in order to see which version of a given passage of Scripture seems to be a better rendition of the original language. Scholars can do this in large part because the science of comparing ancient writings (paleography) has become a very reliable discipline in the 20th century.

Notice that I said that the sources available to the 16th-century translators are "younger" than the Qumran manuscripts. How much younger? The Qumran manuscripts date from about 200 B.C.; the earliest complete Hebrew Old Testament known to the 16th-century translators dates from about the year 930 A.D. This 10th-century manuscript is known as the *Aleppo Codex*.

Since not *every* book of the Old Testament as we have it today has been found at Qumran, the *Aleppo Codex* and other manuscripts dating to the Middle Ages still have their value. In fact, today's scholars still have no *complete* Old Testament manuscript from which to translate that is any older than the *Aleppo Codex*.

So where do our English translations of the Bible come from? Of the six most popular *modern* translations—the *Revised Standard Version* (*RSV*), *New English Bible* (*NEB*), *Good News Bible* (*GNB*), *New International Version* (*NIV*), *New American Bible* (*NAB*) and the *Jerusalem Bible* (*JB*)—all but the *RSV* are new translations.

They represent attempts to translate the ancient originals into today's English (or American English) language. The *RSV* was really a revision of the *Revised Version* (1884) which, to make matters more complicated, was itself a revision of the *King James Version*.

The two Catholic translations (*NAB* and *JB*) are the first significant modern translations made by Catholic scholars from the ancient sources. Prior to these works, Catholic translations into English had been made primarily from the Latin *Vulgate*, which was itself translated from the original languages by St. Jerome beginning in 389 A.D. The modern Protestant translations (*NEB*, *GNB* and *NIV*) are, like their Catholic counterparts, translations from the original languages.

At this point you may be asking, "Why are there 'Catholic' and 'Protestant' translations anyway? Isn't there just *one* Bible?" The answer, unfortunately, is "yes and no." Catholics and Protestants agree when it comes to which books are included in the New Testament. As for the Old Testament, however, Catholics have seven more books (and lengthier sections of two other books) than Protestants have in their Bible.*

How did this situation come about?

Although the bulk of St. Jerome's *Vulgate* translation was made from Hebrew originals, he also included sections from scrolls *written in Greek* which had been included in a famous Greek translation of the Hebrew Bible. This Greek translation—called the *Septuagint*—contained the seven books to which I just referred. The Protestant Reformers of the 16th century decided to use only those Old Testament books originally *written in Hebrew* and thus deleted these seven books from the Bible. The Catholic Church, on the other hand, in accepting and promoting the *Vulgate*, taught that the *Septuagint*—with its seven additional books—was the true Old Testament.

This controversy over which set of books to include in the Old Testament was solidified in 1546 when the bishops of the Catholic Church, meeting at the Council of Trent, established "the ancient Latin *Vulgate*" as the Catholic Church's official

---

*The seven books are Tobit, Judith, Wisdom, Ecclesiasticus, Baruch, and 1 and 2 Maccabees. The lengthier sections in the Catholic Bible are found in Daniel and Esther.

version and—unfortunately—condemned those who did not accept it.

Protestants, perhaps reacting to Catholic hardheadedness, got hardheaded themselves. The seven extra Greek books which Catholics kept in the Old Testament were soon referred to by Protestant scholars in such pejorative language as "the wretched apocrypha." And while the seven books had originally been placed in the back of the first Protestant English Bibles, by 1827 the books were omitted entirely from Protestant English versions. Ever since that time some Protestants have looked on the seven Greek books with perhaps an undue suspicion as to the soundness of their contents.

Interestingly, Martin Luther himself never condemned the books but, on the contrary, said they were "useful and good for reading." Fortunately, the often unchristian polemical warfare surrounding these books is dying down. Many Protestant Bibles today once again include the seven Greek books in a special section entitled "Apocrypha." Catholics, on their part, are no longer required to read only the *Vulgate* or its successors, but may today read *any* reliable translation such as the six I listed above.

Which side was right in the controversy about the books to be included in the Old Testament? It depends on one's viewpoint. The early Church—well before Jerome—had made exclusive use of the Greek version of the Old Testament, both in its readings and its liturgy. Thus, Catholics were "right" in not wanting to deviate from this early Church usage of the *Septuagint* with its seven additional books. Protestants in a sense were also "right," however, in wanting to base the Old Testament strictly on the books which the Jews themselves included in *their* sacred Scriptures. Thus there appears to be merit to both the Catholic and Protestant positions.

The process by which the decision was made concerning which books to include in the *New* Testament took several centuries. Starting about 200 A.D., the Church reached certain tentative conclusions about the 27 books to be included in the New Testament, but there was by no means unanimity. Some respected elders in the Church wanted to exclude the Book of Revelation; some wanted to exclude Hebrews. Others wanted to include books that never made their way into the final New

Testament Canon, such as *The Didache* or the *Shepard* of Hermas.

Decisions on which books to include in the New Testament grew out of the early Christians' shared lives and their shared reflections on the teachings which had been handed down to them from the apostles. Gradually a rough consensus emerged as to which books belonged in the New Testament.

Since these early Christians were part of a community of believers whose shared life in Christ is part of the subject matter of the New Testament, we can't read the New Testament outside of the context of this same communal life of God's people—his Church. We must keep in mind that it is the Church which gave us the Bible, and not the Bible which gave us the Church. Further, while God reveals himself in the Bible, he also reveals himself in the body of people who have given us the Bible and who have cherished and treasured it through the ages.

In addition to disputes about the origins and versions of the Bible, fundamentalists typically disagree with Catholics on various faith doctrines. Let's take a look at certain specific fundamentalist challenges to Catholic beliefs. I will suggest possible responses to these challenges.

CHAPTER THREE

What Catholics Believe—
Responding to Fundamentalist
Challenges

Before focusing on some of the common fundamentalist challenges to Catholic beliefs, I should issue a caution: I don't intend to train anyone in the fundamentalist verse-swapping technique where one spits out a prememorized, "all-proving" Scripture verse to defeat an adversary on a particular point of doctrine.

Fundamentalists have relied for years on this tactic, and Catholics should not even bother trying to match them at this game of scriptural ping-pong. We should understand from the outset that Scripture was never meant to be used in this quiz-show manner with the prize going to the fastest contestant.

Nevertheless, Catholics today need to understand what Scripture has to say (and what it *means*) about various fundamentalist challenges to Catholic beliefs. The only way for Catholics to respond to these fundamentalist challenges is for Catholics themselves to become more educated about the Bible. As we have seen, some fundamentalists will simply not dialogue with Catholics. But for those fundamentalists who do, the only common ground for dialogue is Scripture itself.

'Have You Been Saved?'

For fundamentalists this question is the be-all and end-all of Christianity, the jackpot question, the correct answer to which settles all issues. Catholics in particular are confused as to how to respond to this question. Our theology does not recognize an individual moment of salvation as does the "once-saved, always-saved" fundamentalist theology.

Catholics believe rather in a theology of developing conversion, in line with St. Paul's thought in Philippians 2:12:

> So then, my dearly beloved, obedient as always to my urging, work with anxious concern to achieve your salvation, not only when I happen to be with you, but all the more now that I am absent.

In this verse Paul is obviously speaking to people who have already "accepted Christ" and who consider themselves Christians. Why, if Paul believed in "once-saved, always-saved" theology, did he have to urge the Philippians to "work with anxious concern to achieve your salvation"? The answer is obvious. Paul did not believe in a "one-moment-of-salvation" theology. For Paul, salvation—won for Christians by Jesus' death and resurrection—is an ongoing process which Christians continuously appropriate into their lives.

To understand this concept more deeply—and to make an adequate and intelligent response to fundamentalists on this point—we need to engage in a more concentrated study of Paul's theology.

The starting point for any discussion of Paul's theology about salvation is his understanding of the concepts of *justice*, *faith* and *law*. The Greek word Paul uses in his writings for *justice* is *dikaiosyne*, which in the context is perhaps better translated as "uprightness" or "right-standing." For Paul, as for all Jews, no one is upright but God. The question he addresses in Philippians, Galatians and Romans is how one shares in God's uprightness—that is, how does one become "just"?

The Judaizers whom Paul condemned taught that one can become *just* merely by keeping the dictates of the Law. *Law* is a term used by Paul in several different connotations, the primary one being the teaching preserved in the first five books of the Old Testament and the man-made interpretations of those books.

Paul takes up the process of *justification*—how one is transformed from non-uprightness to uprightness—more fully in Romans. For Paul, the catalyst which transforms the Christian into a condition of justice—and thus of freedom—is faith. The Greek word Paul uses for *faith* is *pistis*. Paul does not mean by this word simply "belief" or "assent." Rather, he means something closer to *acceptance* indicated by *demonstrable signs* in the life of someone who professes belief in Jesus Christ as Savior and Lord. Thus, a person does not become upright before God simply by saying, "I believe!"—although for some persons that may be a valid starting point of faith. To fully express faith in Jesus requires a surrender of one's entire being to the lordship of Jesus.

It would have been inconceivable to Paul for a person to say "Jesus is Lord" without demonstrating in his or her life the love for Jesus and others which such a faith-proclamation presupposes. Paul acknowledged that different persons are at different stages of development in their faith; he knew faith itself is an ongoing process. As the believer's faith grew, Paul expected the believer's deeds of love to grow commensurately.

Let's look at another Pauline term, *redemption*. Redemption is an Old Testament concept as ancient as the Book of Leviticus. In Leviticus 25 the author describes the Israelite right to redeem certain indebted property. A modern example of redemption is found in the pawnshop system. A person who needs money can pawn a personal possession—let's say a watch—and receive money for it. If the person then wants to get the watch back, he or she can "redeem" the watch by paying the pawnbroker's fee within the allotted time. The person thus receives the watch back by way of "redemption."

In Old Testament times people could even pawn themselves if they became heavily indebted, and Leviticus 25:45-55 prescribes certain rules by which a person sold into slavery for debt could be redeemed or liberated.

Old Testament writers began to speak of Yahweh as the redeemer or liberator of his people. They saw Yahweh's ultimate act of redemption and liberation taking place in the Endtime:

> More than sentinels wait for the dawn,
>   let Israel wait for the LORD,
> For with the LORD is kindness
>   and with him is plenteous redemption;
> And he will redeem Israel

from all their iniquities. (Psalm 130:6b-8)

By applying the concept of redemption to Jesus' death and resurrection, Paul is saying that in Jesus God is now bringing humanity to the "plenteous redemption" foretold in the Old Testament. Thus, in Jesus, humanity attains its liberation from sin and becomes free.

Curiously (and contrary to what we might expect), Paul does not call Jesus the "redeemer." He says that Jesus is "our redemption" (1 Corinthians 1:30). This difference in emphasis is explained by Paul in Romans, where he says, "All men are now undeservedly justified by the gift of God, through the redemption wrought *in* Christ Jesus" (3:24, emphasis added). Paul says that it is "*in* Christ Jesus" that redemption is accomplished, and not "*by* Christ Jesus," in order to emphasize that redemption is still continuing and that the final phase of the redemptive act will not be seen until Jesus' Second Coming.

Another word Paul uses to describe the effects of Jesus' death and resurrection is *reconciliation*. Paul says,

> For if, when we were God's enemies, we were reconciled to him by the death of his Son, it is all the more certain that we who have been reconciled will be saved by his life. (Romans 5:10)

By referring to humanity as "God's enemies" Paul does not mean that God despised humanity and was waiting for the day when he would get even for the sins which humanity had committed. This is the false understanding of Jesus' sacrificial death that we talked about in Chapter One—namely, that God sadistically took out his anger against sinful humanity on Jesus by making him go to the cross.

In reality Paul here is referring to God's repulsion at *sin* in the world, not his hatred of *sinners*. Throughout the Old Testament Yahweh is said to be the "all-holy" into whose presence nothing unholy can come. Thus anyone unholy is so distant from God that such a person may as well be God's enemy. God's holiness constantly wars against unholiness in the same sense that light could be said to war with darkness. Thus, by *reconciliation* Paul means not that God has lost his anger for those he hated—since God never had that anger or hatred in the first place—but that God's holiness has now overpowered humanity's unholiness.

"God's enemies" for Paul are those who are "powerless" to become holy (Romans 5:6), while God's adopted children are those who have been empowered with the very holiness of God by having been made upright (justified) by Jesus (Romans 5:9). God's former enemies can now be so bold "as to make God our boast" (Romans 5:11b). The image Paul suggests is that of prisoners of war suddenly being given the run of the country which imprisoned them!

In Romans 5:9 Paul says that humanity will be *saved*. Elsewhere in Romans he refers to *salvation* (1:16; 10:10; 13:11). What does Paul mean by these terms?

Paul saw salvation as the total consequences of God's action in history through Christ. As such, salvation encompasses the other effects of Jesus' death and resurrection we have been discussing, such as redemption, reconciliation and justification.

Yet *salvation* is not simply a catchall term; it has a nuance all its own. For Paul, salvation refers primarily to the Endtime victory reserved by God for his redeemed, reconciled and justified creation. Salvation could thus be said to represent the sum total of God's action throughout time in making his creation holy.

Like other Christians of his day, Paul had a changing awareness of when the final act of salvation—Jesus' Parousia or Second Coming—would take place. In his earlier letters Paul thought Jesus' return would occur shortly, while in later letters his expectation of an imminent Parousia begins to wane. He thus speaks of the Endtime as already being here, yet still to come; he also speaks of *salvation* as being fully realized and yet to come. (Compare, for example, 2 Corinthians 6:2 with 1 Thessalonians 1:9-10.)

Perhaps the best way to reconcile Paul's "here-and-now" perspective on salvation with his "still-to-come" perspective is to contrast what Paul means by salvation with what he means by justification. Paul clearly understood justification to be the *now* result of Jesus' death and resurrection, while he understood salvation to be the *final* product or Endtime result. This becomes clearer if we read Romans 5:9 where Paul says, "Now that we *have been justified* by his blood, it is all the more certain that we *shall be saved* by him from God's wrath" (emphases added).

If a sidewalk preacher in Paul's day had asked him, "Have you been saved, brother?" Paul would have perhaps replied, "I've been justified, brother. My salvation is still taking place." This is the same answer *we* can give today to the fundamentalist's jackpot question.

'Mary Couldn't Have Been a Virgin'

I remember a conversation I once had with a fundamentalist preacher who said rather blithely, "I can't understand how you Catholics believe in Mary's perpetual virginity when the Bible clearly states that she had other children."

I responded, "Please show me in the Bible the words 'Mary had other children.'" The man fumed and fussed for a few minutes as he turned the pages of his Bible, hoping to find the verse that would "prove" my Catholic heresy to be false.

The more he looked the more red-faced he became, for nowhere in the Bible does one find the words "Mary had other children." Fundamentalists often use Scripture passages which do not literally say what fundamentalists insist they say. They then try to incorporate their own interpretations of the passages into Scripture.

What the Bible actually says on this issue appears in such passages as Galatians 1:19, where Paul refers to meeting "James, the brother of the Lord." In Mark 3:31-33 Jesus refers to "my mother and my brothers." In Mark 6:3 we read, "Is this not the carpenter, the son of Mary, a brother of James and Joses and Judas and Simon? Are not his sisters our neighbors here?"

Notice first of all that Mark does not say that Mary is the mother of these brothers of the Lord. That is, Mark does not say, "Is this not the carpenter, the son of Mary, who is also the mother of James and Joses and Judas and Simon?"

To understand the Catholic position on Mary's perpetual virginity, we must understand what the writers of these quoted passages are saying from *their* perspective. In their time the notion of family included not just one's brothers, but also one's cousins and more distant relatives. This Jewish notion of family was very important to them; it developed out of their ancient tribal customs.

Anyone who was a member of one's ancient tribal family

was one's brother or sister. For example, if a Jew was a member of the tribe of Benjamin, all Benjaminites were considered brothers and sisters; if one was a member of the tribe of Judah, all Judahites were seen as brothers and sisters.

In addition, in ancient times there existed the concept of the *extended family*—a larger family unit than merely parents and children—living together and assisting one another with the financial necessities of life. We see this illustrated today in Chinese and Vietnamese families who operate family businesses. Grandmothers and grandfathers, uncles and aunts, cousins, nephews and nieces all work together as the one "family" which owns and operates the family business.

So important to the Jews of Jesus' day was this concept of the extended family that the Hebrew language had not developed a word for "cousin," since one's cousin was thought of as simply another member of the extended family, that is, as a "brother" or "sister." This lack in the Hebrew (and Aramaic) language of a word for "cousin" was acknowledged by the Greek translators of the Hebrew Old Testament as well as by the writers of the Greek New Testament.

Let's look at an illustration of this in Genesis. In order to give the fundamentalists equal time we will use the *King James Version*.

In Genesis 13:8 Abram pleads with Lot, Abram's *nephew*, for peace between them because, as Abram puts it, "we be *brethren*." The Greek word used to translate the Hebrew original is *adelphos*, which in English means simply "brother." This usage of *adelphos* to signify the relationship between uncle and nephew illustrates how the persons who translated the Old Testament into Greek compensated for the deficiency in their language to express distant relationships between relatives.

In Genesis 29:10 we read that Jacob "saw Rachel, the daughter of Laban, his mother's brother." Rachel is thus Jacob's first cousin, and Laban is Jacob's uncle. Yet, in 29:12, Jacob refers to his own uncle as his "brother." Again the Greek word used to translate this distant relationship is *adelphos*.

This usage in the Old Testament of *adelphos* for "cousin" and other more distant relationships was respected by the New Testament writers. By their time it was a common convention to use the Greek *adelphos* to get around the troublesome deficiency in Hebrew for the word *cousin*. These two examples serve to demonstrate how people today can easily distort the meaning intended by scriptural writers by relying on the meaning of English words as they are understood in the 20th century.

Having said this, however, I should point out that there is still the *possibility* of reading the New Testament passages referring to Jesus' brothers and sisters as meaning literally Mary's other children.

To sum up: There is really no scriptural evidence which either proves or disproves the Catholic position that Mary was perpetually a virgin. That belief relies not simply on understanding the Hebrew language's lack of a word for "cousin" and the consequent use of the term "brothers" of Jesus, but also on a strong tradition in the early Church that Mary remained a virgin after Jesus' birth.

This tradition, like so many others in the early Church, was part of the faith community's earliest belief about Jesus. If we cut ourselves off from that early faith community, as fundamentalists do, then of course it is impossible to accept the tradition about Mary which Catholics still cherish today.

'Call No One on Earth Your Father'

Fundamentalists love to quote this passage (Matthew 23:9) to "prove" that Catholic priests, in using the title "Father," go against Jesus' commandment. (Fundamentalists apparently think they get around the problem by calling their male parent "Daddy" or "Papa.")

The title "Father" for priests evolved out of the early Church's shared life. This is shown clearly in Scripture itself, in 1 John 2:1 (again quoting the *King James Version*): "My little children, these things write I unto you, that ye sin not." It is obvious that, if a male elder in the Church refers to his flock as "my little children," his relationship to his flock is that of "father." This respect for early Christian elders was very common in the early Church and was not seen by the early Christians as a contradiction of Jesus' words in Matthew 23:9.

The point of Matthew 23:9 is not to condemn certain labels given to pastors or Christian leaders. Jesus' point, rather, is that Christian elders must not take on the pompous, self-important attitudes of some of the rabbis of Jesus' day. These men behaved as if they were the only means by which a pious Jew could come to know the true Father, Jesus' Father in heaven.

Jesus is saying that the Father in heaven is available to all of his children by a "direct line" through Jesus himself. That is, one's "sonship" with our Father in heaven does not depend on a rabbi, priest or minister. Catholic theology would of course support this concept. Catholic priests do not substitute themselves for God the Father; they act as servants of the Body of Christ in order to minister the gifts given to the Church by the Father through Jesus.

'The Mass Is Not a Sacrifice'

In Hebrews 10:12-14 the writer states that "Jesus offered *one* sacrifice for sins....By *one* offering [Jesus] has forever perfected those who are being sanctified" (emphases added). Fundamentalists use this passage to criticize and condemn the Catholic belief in the sacrifice of the Mass. (The Jack Chick comic books allege that "Catholics have cut these verses out of their Bibles.")

In actuality, fundamentalists misunderstand the Catholic theology of the Mass. The Mass is not a "re-killing" of Jesus or a "re-sacrifice" to the Father, as some fundamentalists would characterize it. Rather, the Mass is the *re-celebration* in time of the *one* sacrifice of Jesus Christ on Calvary. To understand this Catholic position on the Mass more fully, let us explore briefly the scriptural understanding of the Eucharist which is the basis of the Mass.

The Gospel accounts of Jesus' institution of the Eucharist (Matthew 26:26-29; Mark 14:22-25; Luke 22:14-20) revolve around two Old Testament concepts: the Passover and the covenant. The Passover, understood in its original sense, refers to God's action in "passing over" the houses of the Israelites on the night on which he struck down the firstborn of every living creature in Egypt (Exodus 12:12-13). In another sense Passover refers to the Jews' celebration of this same event—the *commemorative ritual* they observe to thank God for sparing them and eventually delivering them from slavery.

The idea of covenant, like that of Passover, also comes

from the Book of Exodus. It refers to the agreement made between Yahweh and his people by which Yahweh became the Israelites' God and they became his special, "chosen" people. The Old Testament is filled with examples of how the people constantly rescinded their promise to be faithful to God, while God nonetheless constantly remained faithful to the people. As a result, God spoke through the prophets to foretell a new covenant—one that God would write on his people's hearts so that in future days his people *would* remain faithful to him (see Jeremiah 31:31-34; Ezekiel 36:26-28).

In both concepts, Passover and covenant, blood plays an important part. On the night of Passover, God knew which houses to "pass over" because the doorposts were marked with the blood of a lamb sacrificed by the Israelites earlier in the evening. Likewise, when Moses ratified the people's covenant with God, he took the blood of two sacrificed bulls and sprinkled it on the people saying, "This is the blood of the covenant which the LORD has made with you in accordance with all of these words of his" (Exodus 24:8).

Thus, by instituting the Eucharist on Passover evening, Jesus wishes to associate his actions with the first Passover event. *He* would be the new Passover lamb, and *his* blood poured out the following afternoon on the cross would be the means of marking God's people for ultimate deliverance from the slavery of sin. By choosing the Passover meal during which to institute the Eucharist, Jesus emphasized that his disciples were to *remember* (Luke 22:19b) the event of his sacrifice in the same way that Jews during their own Passover meals remembered the original event of God's passing over their homes.

By referring to the bread which he distributed as "my body" (Matthew 26:26; Mark 14:22; Luke 22:19), Jesus was telling his disciples that they were associating themselves intimately with his coming *sacrifice* on the cross, in the same way that Jews who ate the Passover lamb in their ritual meal associated themselves with the original Passover *sacrifice*.

By saying of the cup which he shared, "This cup is the new covenant in my blood, which will be shed for you" (Luke 22:20), Jesus was announcing the fulfillment through his sacrificial death of God's Old Testament promise to establish the new covenant prophesied in Jeremiah and Ezekiel. By calling the wine "my blood" (Matthew 26:28; Mark 14:24), Jesus meant that in drinking the wine his disciples would accept in their own lives the terms of this new covenant—God's writing of his law within their hearts—in the same way that the Israelites originally accepted the terms of the old covenant when Moses sprinkled blood on them.

The significance of this Eucharistic institution was much more obvious to the first disciples than it is for us today. Because of our modern tendency to perceive time only in terms of "horizontal time"—expressed in Greek by the word *chronos*—we think of Jesus' actions at the Last Supper as something that *happened* rather than as something that *happens*.

The early Christians, who were more accustomed to living in *kairos* (the Greek word for time in a "vertical," ever-present sense), looked upon their Eucharistic celebrations as "now events." For them Jesus was *fully present* in the breaking of the bread and the sharing of the cup (Luke 24:30-31). For the disciples Jesus' words, "Do this as a remembrance of me" (Luke 22:19), were spoken in the Spirit's power to transform all time into an eternally *present* moment. Jesus' actions were thus another way in which the disciples would "know that I am with you always, until the end of the world" (Matthew 28:20).

The following analogy may help us "educated moderns" to understand the Eucharistic concept of the past's continuity into the present. If we take a rubber band and mark it with a white chalk dot, it is obvious where that dot was originally placed. Yet, if we stretch the rubber band, we can see a long band of white chalk, filling up a space much longer than the space occupied by the original dot. In the same way Jesus' institution of the Eucharist and his *one* sacrifice on the cross are events which, though occupying a single "dot" in time, also pervade all other moments of time in which they are remembered and celebrated.

'One Is Saved by Faith Alone'

In Romans 10:9 we read, "For if you confess with your lips that Jesus is Lord, and believe in your heart that God raised him from the dead, you will be saved." Many fundamentalists read this passage as something of a "password" to salvation, a formula which opens the gates of heaven. This type of thinking displays the fundamentalist mechanistic approach to salvation. It's almost as if one simply needs to say the correct formula, stick one's quarter in the machine and pull the handle, and out pops salvation.

It is necessary to contrast this mechanistic approach to salvation with our earlier discussion of Paul's own understanding of faith. Paul saw faith as acceptance of Jesus with one's entire being (not simply with the tongue) shown by one's actions apart from and *in addition to* the words one has repeated.

This remark lies at the root of another perennial controversy between fundamentalists and Catholics. Fundamentalists accuse Catholics of being "under law" while fundamentalists consider themselves to be "under grace." They say that Catholics believe in salvation by works rather than by faith.

I am reminded here of the fundamentalist preacher who told me that everything Mother Teresa of Calcutta does is simply "dead works" with no effect on her salvation. I suggested to the man that he consider Matthew 7:21-24: "None of those who cry out, 'Lord, Lord,' will enter the Kingdom of God but only the one who does the will of my Father in heaven." Jesus very specifically cautions against a salvation-by-words mentality.

Catholics believe just as much as fundamentalists that "a man is justified by faith apart from observance of the law" (Romans 3:28). The difference between Catholics and fundamentalists lies in what happens next. Catholics believe that good works must flow from one's faith, as a sign of one's faith in action. We accept fully James's advice:

> My brothers, what good is it to profess faith without practicing it? Such faith has no power to save one, has it? If a brother or sister has nothing to wear and no food for the day, and you say to them, "Good-bye and good luck! Keep warm and well fed," but do not meet their bodily needs, what good is that? So it is with the faith that does nothing in practice. It is thoroughly lifeless....Be assured, then, that faith without works is as dead as a body without breath.
> (James 2:14-17, 26)

Fundamentalists tend to base everything on their one "faith proclamation." Once that all-encompassing "I believe!" is said, it's almost as if—for some fundamentalists—the only significant thing left to do is die and go to heaven. Fundamentalist theology revolves around the *past moment* of that faith proclamation, whereas Catholic theology keeps pointing ahead toward the future, toward faith in action, toward ever greater service for our brothers and sisters.

'Show Me the Pope, the Catholic Church and the Trinity in the Bible'

Fundamentalists are right in saying that *pope, Catholic Church* and *Trinity* are words not found in the Bible. One doesn't find the names *Martin Luther* and *John Calvin* in the Bible either, but that does not mean that the Holy Spirit did not work through Luther and Calvin to form the latter-day Church. Lutherans and Presbyterians would not alter their belief on the basis of the missing names!

Catholics do not believe that divine revelation is limited to the pages of Scripture, nor do Catholics believe that the Holy Spirit quit guiding the Church after the Bible was completed. We believe, rather, that through the Holy Spirit's action in history, the Spirit has developed fuller understandings of doctrines which are present in "seed form" in the Bible. Papal primacy, the Trinity and our present understanding of Church are among these.

1) The papacy

The word *pope* comes not from the Bible, but from the Latin word *papa* (or the Greek word *pappas*). This was a common colloquial expression the early Church used to express respect for pastors and elders. The title *papa* in reality was used for *all* early bishops, not simply for the Bishop of Rome.

Gradually, however, the title came to be used solely by the Bishop of Rome to refer to himself and, by the fourth and fifth centuries, the word *pope* was reserved by the other bishops of the Church for the Bishop of Rome. Was this human work or God's work? I suppose the way in which one answers that question depends on whether one is Protestant or Catholic, and it is not my intention here to settle the long debate that has arisen over that question.

The point I wish to make is that the lack of the word *pope* in the Bible does not "prove" that the Holy Spirit did not develop the role of the papacy for the Church. The Holy Spirit works through history to achieve the divine purpose. Catholics should understand, however, that this works both ways.

In other words, the Holy Spirit could very well change the character of the papacy as we know it today, so that in the future the Pope could share more of his authority as presiding elder of the bishops by taking other bishops more into his counsel in making decisions. In fact, since Pope John XXIII we have seen a definite move in the direction of more collegiality among the Pope and his brother bishops.

Catholics should not be fundamentalists themselves when it comes to the papacy, but should admit that the Holy Spirit can reform and reshape the external manifestation of papal primacy and adapt it to the needs of modern times. In many ways the papacy today is simply a vestige of its medieval form and, many would argue, there is no need to continue the medieval trappings into the 20th century.

2) The Trinity

Although the concept of three persons in one God is clearly present in seed form both in Paul's and John's writings, the first use of the word itself occurred about the year 180 A.D. Bishop Theophilus of Antioch was writing to a friend, Autolykos, and in the resulting treatise of the same name (*Autolykos*) he referred to the three persons in the one God by using the word *trinitas*. Theophilus's thinking was clearly a progression of the thinking of both St. Paul and St. John, even though neither biblical writer used the word *Trinity*.

Once again we see that the understanding of the truths of the faith continued to expand after the last word of the Bible was written.

Interestingly, Bishop Theophilus thought and wrote in the same community of Christians which was deliberating on the books it was going to accept as the normative New Testament. He would hardly have invented a term which he found to be inconsistent with his contemporary Church's understanding of the New Testament.

3) The Catholic Church

This phrase was first used by Ignatius, Bishop of Antioch, in about the year 115. Ignatius was being transported to Rome for execution because of his Christian faith. Along the route to Rome, Ignatius wrote seven letters to other Christian communities in which he expressed his understanding of the developing Christian Church. In one of these letters he used the phrase *Catholic Church* to refer to the primitive Christian Church. (Ignatius also invented the word *Christianity*.)

Some members of the community in which Ignatius lived knew the apostle John personally; it is thus unlikely that Ignatius would have made up a conception of the Church of which John's disciples and contemporaries would have disapproved.

In using the phrase *Catholic Church*, Ignatius was simply expressing what was already an accepted fact—that the individual Church communities scattered across the entire expanse of the Roman Empire regarded themselves as catholic or universal, that is, as bound together in a common body.

Examples of the early catholicity of the Church are seen in the hospitality and respect which was shown to traveling Christians (such as Ignatius himself). The catholicity of Christian life in the early second century is further illustrated by the extensive letter-writing which took place between one Christian community and another.

Further, early shared creedal statements were passed from community to community. These gradually culminated in the great formal expressions of the shared Catholic faith at the councils of the fourth and fifth centuries. In addition, the catholicity of the Church was reflected in its universal acceptance of the rite of Baptism as the means of initiation into the Body of Christ and of the Eucharist as the central act of Christian worship. We see this exemplified in a letter which Bishop Polycarp of Smyrna wrote sometime prior to 156 A.D. Polycarp comments that he celebrated the Eucharist in Rome in essentially the same manner in which he celebrated it back home in Smyrna.

Finally, the early Church demonstrated its catholicity in its reliance on the apostolic tradition as the bedrock of authentic Christian doctrine. This apostolic tradition—as continued in the episcopal nature of Church leadership—was never seen as contrary to the New Testament, since the New Testament was seen as part and parcel *of* the apostolic tradition. In the early

Church the appeal to the authority of the apostles went hand in hand with the appeal to the authority of the New Testament. The early Christians did not conceive of the Church as based solely on either apostolic tradition or the Bible; they saw the Church as founded on *both*.

To summarize, then, although such words as *pope*, *Trinity* and *Catholic Church* do not appear in the Bible, these words undoubtedly express constituent elements in the life of the same faith community which gave us the New Testament.

'Are You Ready for the Rapture?'

We will consider one final fundamentalist idea which we hear a lot about today. *The Rapture*—a term found nowhere in the Bible—is something that is completely mysterious to most Catholics. What is the Rapture and what is the origin of this fundamentalist invention? The answer to this question lies in a brief discussion of the Book of Revelation and in an analysis of the fundamentalists' literal reading of that book.*

The portion of the Book of Revelation about which there is probably the most disagreement among Christians is Chapter 20. That chapter describes a thousand-year period when Satan will be "chained up." After this millennium period, during which Christians will "reign with Christ" (see 20:4), "Satan will be released from his prison. He will go out to seduce the nations in all four corners of the earth..." (20:7-8).

The Catholic Church teaches that the "thousand years" of Revelation 20 does not mean that there will be an earthly reign of Christ, at some time in the future, between now and the last day of history. As to what the thousand years *does* mean, there are a variety of opinions among Catholic biblical scholars. Perhaps the ancient view of St. Augustine is still the most common: The thousand-year period refers to all of time after the death and resurrection of Jesus. The "first resurrection" of Revelation 20:5-6 thus refers to the condition of Christians after they are baptized. The "second death" of 20:6 refers to the

---

*The following paragraphs are quoted substantially verbatim from my article in *Today's Parish*, with the kind approval of Twenty-Third Publications, the publisher of that periodical.

condition of those who live in the Christian era (the "thousand years") but who do not accept Baptism. This Catholic position on the meaning of Revelation 20 is shared by many Protestant denominations.

Fundamentalists, on the other hand, interpret Revelation 20 literally and believe that there will be an actual thousand-year period during which Jesus will reign as king over the entire earth. Among these fundamentalists there are varying shades of opinion as to how this will happen. One of these opinions, given the unwieldy name of "dispensational premillennialism," holds that when the millennium begins, the Church will be "raptured out" of the world to heaven while Jesus establishes his earthly reign.

Proponents of this school of thought believe that during the millennium many Jews will accept the salvation of Jesus. These Jews will make up the New Israel, which will later join the Church in heaven. Premillennialists do not believe, as do most Christians, that the *Church* is the New Israel—the new People of God which has inherited the promises made to the Israel of the Old Testament. They believe instead that the promises made in the Old Testament to Israel must be literally fulfilled through the Jewish people.

Since the word *rapture* appears nowhere in Scripture, how did the word come into common usage among fundamentalists? The word itself was first used as a marginal note in a famous Protestant study Bible. Through the years so many people used this study Bible that the term became as common in some circles as the actual passage to which it was applied: "Then we, the living, the survivors, will be caught up with them in the clouds to meet the Lord in the air" (1 Thessalonians 4:17).

This passage, too, was interpreted literally, and the prospect of standing on a cloud with the Lord in the air was looked forward to as being exhilarating, thrilling—rapturous. (*Webster's New Collegiate Dictionary* defines rapture as "a state or experience of being carried away by overwhelming emotion.") Reading 1 Thessalonians 4:17 in conjunction with Revelation 20, these Christians concluded that the entire Church would be taken to meet Jesus in the air ("raptured out") at the start of the millennium.

While God may in fact have things planned so that we all meet Jesus in the air on the last day, the rapturist interpretation of 1 Thessalonians 4:17 misses the point of what Paul was getting at when he used the phrase "in the air." We must remember that the writers of the New Testament did not have our knowledge of physics and astronomy. For example, they thought that the earth was the center of creation and that the sun was "above" the earth and rotated around it. They didn't know as we do that there is no "above" or "below" when one refers to the relative positions of the sun and earth.

Further, they believed that spiritual beings lived above the earth in the air. The author of Ephesians, for example, wrote: "Our battle is not against human forces but against...the evil spirits in *regions above*" (Ephesians 6:12, emphasis added). Thus, Paul's purpose in saying that the elect would meet the Lord "in the air" was to teach that on the Last Day God will have defeated all the powers of evil; he will have vanquished them in their own domain—"the air."

The important point for Paul was *that* God will be victorious on the Last Day, not *where* he will be victorious. If Paul were alive today and discovered that spirits don't really live "in the air," his basic teaching would not change. He would simply use a different image to express that teaching.

What do these reflections on the rapturist school of the Endtime have to say about our daily walk with the Lord? It may seem to us that it doesn't make much difference whether we accept the Catholic or the premillennial viewpoint concerning the Endtime. After all, despite what *our* opinion may be, God's plan for the Endtime will prevail anyway. Yet, our viewpoint does have a significance which is more than academic.

If we were to adopt the rapturist viewpoint, there is the possibility that we could become unduly passive in our relationship with those around us—both Christian and non-Christian. We could tend to sit back and say, "The world is sure going to the dogs. Why bother fighting it? Jesus will come soon and give all these sinners what they deserve." This seems to summarize the attitude of some fundamentalists, whose entire "ministry" appears to be devoted to warning others of their impending damnation—almost as if they revel in the prospect.

This attitude was hardly Jesus' attitude. He certainly didn't revel over the prospect of damnation for those who refused to accept him. Nor did he withdraw from combat with evil by leaving it up to his Father to win the fight for him. In the Garden of Gethsemane he did not say, "I think I'll sit back now and watch as my Father sends his angels out to defeat my enemies." Jesus walked right into the face of evil, confronted it and defeated it.

We are called to continue Jesus' mission, including the work of transforming sin into love and death into life. This experience will hardly be a rapturous one, but—judging from the lives of those who have wholeheartedly shared this ministry with Jesus—it will certainly be a joyous one.

We can hardly carry out our Christian mission if we withdraw from the field, passively relying on the Father to win the battle for us. And if we focus too much on the end point of our journey—on the *heavenly* rapture that awaits us all—we may miss the joy of the intervening journey.

Therefore, while we should always keep one eye open for the Lord's final victory at the end of time, we should not fail to live in the present. A good response to the fundamentalist question, "Are you ready for the Rapture?" might be, "I am so busy with the Lord's work that I haven't given it much thought."

Conclusion

We eventually come to a point in our disagreements with fundamentalists where debate about doctrine keeps us from attending to the work of building up the Kingdom of God on earth. Instead of worrying so much about who's right, we should be more concerned about living in right relationship with one another. Ultimately, the best response to fundamentalists—or to anyone else who challenges our Catholic beliefs—is not words, but the lived example of Christian love.

If our lives as Catholics were such that fundamentalists had to say, "See how those Catholics love one another, all other people and God's entire creation," Catholics would eventually have no fundamentalist challenge with which to contend. The ultimate solution to fundamentalism lies not in improving fundamentalists, but in improving ourselves.

By doing this we make the best response possible to the fears and insecurities which are expressed in fundamentalist attacks on Catholicism. We should always base our response to the fundamentalist challenge on these words from Scripture:

> The man who claims to be in light,
> hating his brother all the while,
> is in darkness even now.
> The man who continues in the light
> is the one who loves his brother;
> there is nothing in him to cause a fall.

But the man who hates his brother is in darkness,
He walks in shadows,
not knowing where he is going,
since the dark has blinded his eyes. (1 John 2:9-11)

I will leave it to God to judge whether it is fundamentalists or Catholics who are "in darkness." It seems to me, however, that the methods used by certain fundamentalists to challenge Catholic beliefs have already been judged in Scripture. All Christians, in approaching other Christians of differing beliefs, might do well to meditate on this scriptural judgment:

Love has no room for fear;
rather, perfect love casts out all fear.
And since fear has to do with punishment,
love is not yet perfect in one who is afraid. (1 John 4:18)

2